1982

VILLAGE SCHOOLS

A FUTURE FOR THE PAST?

Sam
Gardner

VILLAGE SCHOOLS

A FUTURE FOR THE PAST?

Photographed by Jon Wyand
Foreword by Ronald Blythe

Evans Brothers Limited
London

Published by Evans Brothers Limited,
Montague House, Russell Square,
London, WC1B 5BX

Typesetting by South Bucks Typesetters Ltd,
Beaconsfield, Bucks.

Foreword © Ronald Blythe, 1980

ISBN 0 237 44994 3   PRA 6600

Acknowledgements
The author wishes to thank the following for their assistance and
encouragement during the preparation of this book:

Graham and Anne Baxendale; Mrs E. Chalmers; Ted Ferguson;
Mrs Vera Fleming; Faith Harrison; Anne Hoare;
George W. John MBE; Colin and Helen Molyneux; Molly and
Ray Stiles; Trevor Wood; the Education Authorities for the
schools herein and the staff of the 235 schools visited.

All photographs on Kodak Tri-X film.

Printed by G. A. Pindar and Son Limited, Scarborough

For my late father and mother

Introduction

The average Victorian rural school, whether in use or not, or even if it has been recently transformed into a hard-lined house, is a powerful piece of architecture. Just on a century old now, with its foundations in the 1870 Education Act and its silent bell casting a shadow across the television aerial, it straddles in such a comparatively short space of time two vastly different concepts of childhood. Forget the simple charm of the tall classrooms and concentrate on the group photographs of circa 1900, 1912 and 1922, and there you will see, not only another generation but almost another race! Compare the faces and bodies of these mysterious little sitters with those of today's pupils if you want to understand the building. Its strict limitations have an almost lyrical appeal for us now which would have amazed the village. Awe, yes. A vaguely Anglican uplift and certainty, possibly. But to draw a sentimental satisfaction from its sharp façade and durable contents—how such an attitude would have astonished our grandparents! As for the many literary recollections of the first fifty or so years of popular education in the countryside, they mostly vere between the indignant and the bemused, although lit occasionally by a writer's recognition that were it not for some percipient village schoolteacher his life would have followed a far less rewarding course.

Both the great virtue and the great disaster of countless village schools used to be the static nature of their staff. When a lifetime's loyal service to a community by rector, teacher or doctor was the admired thing, the chances were evenly divided between its being a disaster or a blessing for two or three generations. A long innings at the blackboard left an indelible mark on a place. Those fascinating documents, the log-books, are subtle records of slow progress or no progress, of plodding obedience to the syllabus and strict observance of the annual cycle of Christian and patriotic feasts (the two getting strangely confused so that eventually Empire Day and Armistice Day outdid the solemnities of Good Friday and All Saints); of new brooms pushing their way into ruts, of gallant battles by Miss or Sir against weather, child-toil, fearful epidemics and a thousand and one economic factors threatening regular attendance, and, now and then on the copper-plate page ('thin up, thick down'), little glimpses of real inspiration.

Opening such a log-book at once sets up what was once among the most familiar village sounds, the rhythmic baying of hundreds of young voices as generations of vanished country children 'say' their lessons. People in search of ancient rural noises often forget this regular metronomic infant chanting of Faith, Arithmetic, Duty and English, and how it dominated the adult community round about; the same inflexions for alphabet, Commandments, dates and tables, the same little tricks for grasping the same little facts.

Joshua the son of Nun
And Caleb the son of Jephunneh
Were the only two
That ever got through
To the Land of Milk and Honey.

It echoed up into the varnished rafters and out into the fields, and as it was usually necessary for two different classes of 'little 'uns' and Big Boys to carry on two different sayings of lessons in the one rocking room, the chants would grind one against the other as Scripture fought to get some kind of oral edge on Sums. Such daily antiphons were spaced out with dead silences. No talking. No fidgeting. No breathing if you could help it. To bring about a pin-dropping quiet in a class of eighty pupils was a much admired achievement in a teacher and considered to be the acme of professional ability. Not much of what was gathered by rote was analysed, for this would have imperilled the confidence of the recitation and thus, eventually, of village society itself. One still meets old country people who are word-perfect in great stretches of language covering psalms and songs and rules and regulations. They are grateful for 'having got it by heart', as teacher said they one day would be.

There were many more village schools before the 1870s than is now popularly supposed, some of them offering eccentric and very interesting curricular as charitable squire or loving clergyman brought in a graduate to give the parish children simple versions of the kind of education they'd had themselves. Thomas Hardy went to such a school and was indeed the first boy to enter its doors after the lady of the manor had built it. He said that 'she made it her hobby, till it was far superior to an ordinary village school'. When a Suffolk rector founded a school at Debach, it became the habit of the poet Edward FitzGerald, who lived nearby, to read stories from the *Iliad* and the *Odyssey* to the children, and to lend them books. Many of these schools were not housed in special buildings but in corners of the church, the vicarage, etc. Bewick was allowed to practise drawing by chalking pictures all over the church

floor; and fragments of such education in the form of sand-tables, inkwells fitted to pews and alphabets and multiplication tables painted on vestry walls are still to be found all over Britain.

But it is the relics of early state education which intrigue us now. For some time after the last war these schools lacked any kind of charm and were even found hateful, as being remnants of an all too easily remembered poverty, both physical and intellectual, and sometimes of brutality. Those who attended them breathed a sigh of relief when they were closed down and their own children bussed to new sunny Primaries miles away. However, as with all things, the day of re-evaluation has dawned and now being too far off, socially speaking, to feel the smart of what so many of them represented, or to see in what might be called their iconography anything more than a general historic appeal, we acknowledge that a solidly-built, old village school with its quota of between fifty and a hundred children is an asset indeed. They are even attracting exceptionally good staff, including young headteachers who are realising that in such settings they have the chance to be educators in the fullest and most personal sense. Neither are there now such efforts to disguise their stark lines, fruitless though such efforts usually were, for architecture like this defies any watering-down or softening process. It can sprout amenities but it cannot be fundamentally transformed into a later ideal. Put in false wooden ceilings to assist the central heating, but they will never obliterate the soaring reality of what is above them, the high-pitched sounding-board

against which all that basic learning was aimed.

Take the windows which, if you were under twelve, you would need to stand on a desk to see out. They were not placed thoughtlessly so, but to cut out distraction. A bird or a tapping branch might drag young eyes to what was happening beyond the pane, but nothing more. Take the green and cream paint divided by the black dado; this used to be the colour-scheme for every kind of public institution, its utility and special restfulness being scientifically proved they said. As the academic year advanced, 'handwork' from the syllabus appeared along the dado with liturgical precision, yellow paper crocuses, chalky catkins, 'Our House', carefully-ruled Union Jacks, handwriting with Top Marks and neatly-shaded pencil drawings of cubes and pyramids. Above these triumphs hung framed oleographs and prints of happy natives bringing in the banana and tea harvests, and Lord Roberts, General Gordon and the Queen herself with her heavy gaze. Below the dado the brown distemper was flaky and chipped as it met the scrubbed floor with its crevasses damp with Lysol and its nails polished like diamonds by hobs and tips and blakeys, and especially by having the massive cast-iron feet of the desks dragged across them. Take also the huge black-bellied stoves which when fully roused could make your spit jump a foot; its function was less to keep the school warm than to dry out scores of sodden boots and coats for the long tramp home. Take, most of all, teacher's shiny yellow desk and stool on their dais; they were her throne, her tribunal, which to approach, even with a bunch of Michaelmas daisies,

let alone a sin, made one feel quite giddy. Ultimate power presided there. Take the deal cupboards with their precious stock which had to be counted over and over again; slate-pencils, stone bottles of Stephen's ink, pins, carbolic soap, 'school' nibs, coloured beads and, most of all, paper. To spoil a piece of paper was unforgivable, so dreadful an action was it that it took real nerve to write your name on the top of a clean page. To blot your copy-book—what a fate!

The church excluded, no other structure in the village carries with it such a mixture of bitter-sweet overtones as its old school. Jon Wyand's marvellous photographs are all reminders, all evocations. We shall never be able to exorcise these places of what once happened in them, but we are now sufficiently distanced in time from their early days to find them intriguing, even just the thing we need for the future.

Ronald Blythe 1980

Inspector's Report

This happy little country school is
attended by twenty-one children,
seven of whom belong to one family.
It has a charming homely atmosphere.
The headmistress is devoted to her
work and the children repay her
interest in them as individuals with
ready co-operation and eagerness to
learn. They evidently enjoy coming to
school.

The different groups in which ages
range from four to thirteen years are
managed with resourcefulness that
keeps all interested and busily
engaged and ensures steady and good
progress.
30 MAY 1938 MICHAELSTOWE,
CORNWALL

Number present seventy-eight of all ages, between three and fifteen and myself the only teacher! 27 FEBRUARY 1901 MUNSLOW, SHROPSHIRE

Today several children were annoyed because they thought I opened too early and even told *me* the right time, it plainly shows that a few of them have been allowed to do as *they* like.
15 NOVEMBER 1922 MICHAELSTOWE, CORNWALL

No holiday! ! ! Very few children in school this morning. It is a great loss to the master to keep the school on a general holiday as the average for the week will be lowered considerably hence the average for the year will be lowered and that will mean a loss to the master of 6s. a head.
1 JANUARY 1872 DERWEN, CLWYD

The attendance is somewhat affected by an otter hunt in the Wharfe.
20 AUGUST 1900 THRESHFIELD, N. YORKSHIRE

Snow and sleet. Six children were
sent home too wet to remain at the
school. Many of those remaining
were allowed to stay near the fire
their boots being taken off and placed
to dry.
18 JANUARY 1924 LITTLE BYTHAM,
LINCOLNSHIRE

The school bell being out of order
many of the children were late this
morning as they usually linger by the
wayside till they hear it.
19 JUNE 1874 CHISLET, KENT

To Thos. Thatcher Hanging Bell 9d.
846 KILMERSDON, SOMERSET

In order to preserve discipline was compelled to punish (four children) for fastening doors and refusing to open them when desired by the Master. This seems to have been what was called 'Barring Out Day' a custom which when yielded to severely affects discipline.
22 NOVEMBER 1878 GLANTON, NORTHUMBERLAND

The answers to enquiries respecting absentees are 'creadleing', 'rocking creadle', 'helping Mother', 'bad', 'has to take Father's dinner', 'bad shoes', 'brambling', 'Mother's washing', 'tatering'.
3 OCTOBER 1876 BOOSEBECK, CLEVELAND

The attendance has fallen considerably
as a result of two Zeppelin raids in
the night on the 2nd and 6th insts.
Forty-five per cent of the children
spent the night in the Mines and
twenty-five per cent never went to bed.
7 APRIL 1916 MARGROVE PARK,
CLEVELAND

'Charity children' the sign of a
charity school at the beginning of the
eighteenth century.

Monday alone to be allowed as a holiday! All work and no play will make Jack a dull boy! The holidays allowed in this school are not worth having.

22 DECEMBER 1871 DERWEN, CLWYD

Twelve-thirty. Motor car passed round the school from the Rectory road to Lane End going quite thirty miles per hour. Fortunately the children were in school.
24 JANUARY 1910 CORSLEY, WILTSHIRE

The wet weather and the want of shoes among other causes have kept several children away from school this week.
26 FEBRUARY 1876 ARLINGHAM, GLOUCESTERSHIRE

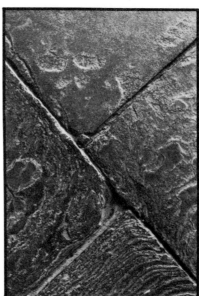

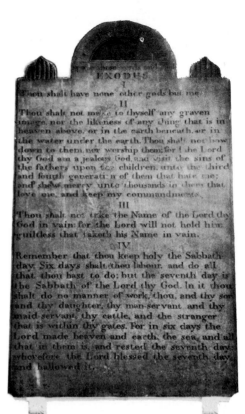

EXODUS

I

Thou shalt have none other gods but me.

II

Thou shalt not make to thyself any graven image, nor the likeness of any thing that is in heaven above, or in the earth beneath, or in the water under the earth. Thou shalt not bow down to them, nor worship them; for I the Lord thy God am a jealous God, and visit the sins of the fathers upon the children, unto the third and fourth generation of them that hate me; and shew mercy unto thousands in them that love me, and keep my commandments.

III

Thou shalt not take the Name of the Lord thy God in vain: for the Lord will not hold him guiltless that taketh his Name in vain.

IV

Remember that thou keep holy the Sabbath day. Six days shalt thou labour, and do all that thou hast to do: but the seventh day is the Sabbath of the Lord thy God. In it thou shalt do no manner of work, thou, and thy son and thy daughter, thy man-servant and thy maid-servant, thy cattle, and the stranger that is within thy gates. For in six days the Lord made heaven and earth, the sea, and all that in them is, and rested the seventh day: wherefore the Lord blessed the seventh day, and hallowed it.

Report by Inspector of Religious Education. In this remote spot and small school *work of real value* is going forward and the staff, who find here and there among their scholars an almost virgin field, are alive to the urgency and importance of their efforts. The school opening exercises could perhaps be made somewhat more impressive and arresting in a simple way; and the cultural power of hymn singing might be more consistently pursued.
28 JUNE 1923 CURRIDGE, BERKSHIRE

I ntimation received that North Riding Education Committee have granted £7 ($\frac{1}{3}$ costs) towards the piano on condition that the remaining £14 is contributed locally.
13 NOVEMBER 1908 CARLIN HOW, CLEVELAND

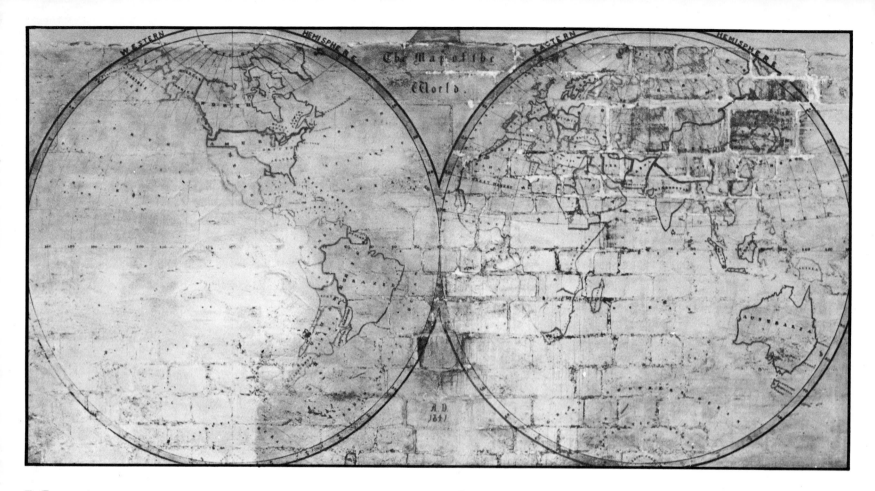

Mistress gave a Geography lesson to standard II this afternoon on 'form and motions of the earth', aided by an orange and a lighted candle. Children appear much interested and amused.
7 FEBRUARY 1877 MORLEY
ST. BOTOLPH, NORFOLK

Standard III have now read the *Voyage round the coast of England* for the third time. An examination today elicited the following answers.
'What is Whitby famous for?' 'Things'.
'What town stands on the Humber?' 'Newcastle'.

'What is Brighton famous for?' 'Iron Goods'.
In fact the amount of intelligence displayed was the smallest possible.
7 NOVEMBER 1881 WOOTTON, OXFORDSHIRE

A man called today to see about the clock, said it required oiling etc. and set it going. It stopped almost directly the man went.
18 OCTOBER 1878 KIRBY BEDON, NORFOLK

My cupboard space is inadequate
there being only a library cupboard
and a stock cupboard in the school.
The latter has been damaged by rats
and mice and is much too damp for
good books.
28 OCTOBER 1931 GODSHILL,
HAMPSHIRE

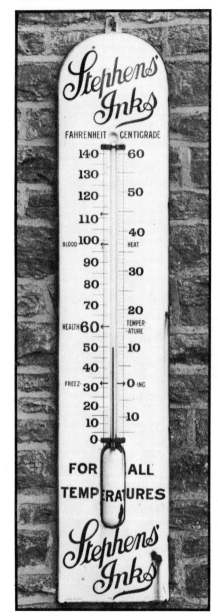

The ink was frozen on Monday so pencils were used until it thawed.
FEBRUARY 1912 CARDINGTON, BEDFORDSHIRE

'Civil Service' type of writing was adopted, may cause confusion for a time.
24 MAY 1894 GLANTON, NORTHUMBERLAND

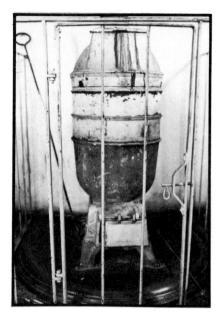

Heavy rain storm . . . twenty-seven out of sixty-nine present have had to be placed around fires in order to have their stockings etc. dried.
12 NOVEMBER 1912 SHILBOTTLE, NORTHUMBERLAND

The stove smoked so badly this morning that the children had to go into the playground to allow the fire to burn up a little and the room to clear. It was with great difficulty that the hymn was sung and the prayers repeated as all in the room were choked with smoke through which the children at the back of the room could not be seen.
21 APRIL 1937 MELBURY ABBAS, DORSET

Temperature in main room at 9am with two good fires going was minus two degrees centigrade.
29 FEBRUARY 1904 GLANTON, NORTHUMBERLAND

The room has not reached 42° during the whole of this week.
15 DECEMBER 1916 CLIVE, SHROPSHIRE

As there is a 'blackout' at the school, fires cannot be lit until 8.30 and the rooms are not warm.
6 JANUARY 1941 ADISHAM, KENT

My Lords are not prepared to admit that instruction in Drawing is unsuitable for boys to be employed in Agriculture – training of the hand and eye by drawing cannot fail to be of use in many operations of husbandry.
APRIL 1891 PUNNETTS TOWN, W. SUSSEX

Word building in infants class seems to be grasped by the majority although the Phonetic method has been substituted for the alphabetic.
4 DECEMBER 1896 BEWHOLME, HUMBERSIDE

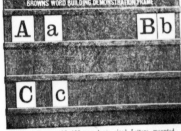

For disturbing a wasps' hive and pushing girls into it so that several were stung, four strokes on each hand.
25 JULY 1911 ASHURST, W. SUSSEX

. . . great difficulty in fixing their minds long upon one subject. A little stirring up with something rather sharper than words might possibly prove of considerable service; but I suppose it won-ner do.
6 DECEMBER 1872 MUSLOW, SHROPSHIRE

A Victorian 'attention-getter'.

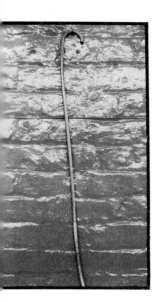

R e bad spelling . . . is the worst
but he has such bad hands caused by
the cold winds that I cannot punish
him for his work.
27 FEBRUARY 1891 ARLINGHAM,
GLOUCESTERSHIRE

I intend to inflict no more corporal
punishment, the stick has today been
burnt.
1 MARCH 1909 THRESHFIELD,
N. YORKSHIRE

The older children were taken to
Aust Cliff this morning to watch for
aeroplanes expected on their way to
Filton. Other observations were made
and recorded in the exercise books.
26 JULY 1911 REDWICK AND
NORTHWICK, AVON

Last week the rector provided a
foot ball which the boys are highly
delighted with – in fact I think it is
just now improving the attendance.
21 MARCH 1899 MUNSLOW,
SHROPSHIRE

Played with the children at Ball a
game which they thoroughly enjoy
particularly that with the foot.
6 MARCH 1868 GARTON ON THE
WOLDS, HUMBERSIDE

In accordance with His Majesty's
gratuitous wish that the school should
be closed for a week to commemorate
the coronation the children were given
a week's holiday. 'Long live the King'.
16 JUNE 1911 GARTON ON THE WOLDS,
HUMBERSIDE

Free milk scheme began today.
6 JANUARY 1947 CAMROSE SOUTH,
PEMBROKESHIRE

I find it quite a waste of time and labour for the boys to continue their gardening lessons on Wednesday afternoons as the rabbits have become such a pest and destroy all the children's produce. As a substitute for this subject I am taking English composition.
6 MAY 1931 CURRIDGE, BERKSHIRE

The children were also warned against writing on doors, profane language and failing to turn off the water tap.
27 OCTOBER 1880 GLANTON, NORTHUMBERLAND

Called for a show of pencils and punished one boy who had already lost the piece given him yesterday.
25 JUNE 1863 ARRETON, ISLE OF WIGHT

Grooves worn by children sharpening their slate pencils.

Numbers very low today. It being St. Valentine Day it is a custom here for children to go to the farmers for pence, etc.
14 FEBRUARY 1879 KIRBY BEDON, NORFOLK

Today being Michaelmas day there has been the customary removals in the village involving much absence among the children and the final leaving of at least eleven children.
11 OCTOBER 1907 MORLEY ST. BOTOLPH, NORFOLK

55

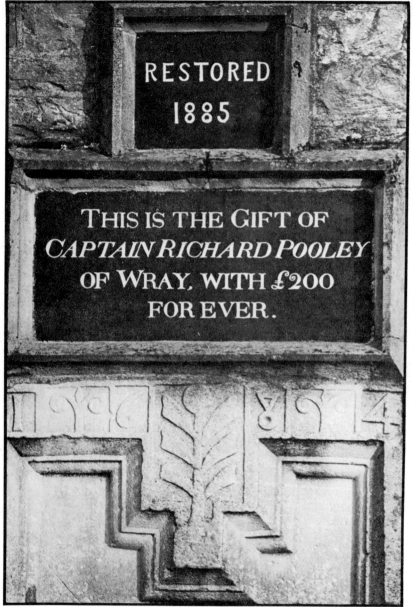

Orders for the better Government of said school, Item 2.

That every Whit Munday shall be ye day of a General Account at wch time ye new treasurer shall entertain those subscribers who shall then appear at his own house with two Dishes of Meat, ye one boyled and the other Roast and such liquor as his house affords.
1 MAY 1718 CHEW STOKE, AVON

Details of annual government grant towards running of the school, paid according to average attendance over school year.
Average attendance
Boys 66   Girls 51.1   Total 117.1

1 Fixed Grant	9/-
2 Variable Grant	4/-
3 Needlework Grant	1/-
4 Singing Grant	1/-
	15/- x 117
	£87 15 0
Grant under article 102	2 0 0
	89 15 0

30 JUNE 1892 SKINNINGROVE, CLEVELAND

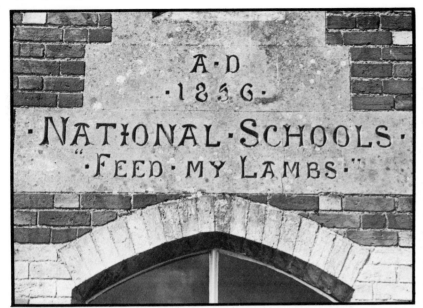

A·D
·1856·
·NATIONAL·SCHOOLS·
"·FEED·MY·LAMBS·"

B C
1835

THIS SCHOOL WAS ERECTED AFTER A PLAN OF THE
PRINCE CONSORT
BY
QUEEN VICTORIA
1904

At the request of the managers
the dinner hour interval has been
extended to 1.15pm to allow a little
extra time for children attending the
Soup Kitchen.
27 JUNE 1921 CARLIN HOW,
CLEVELAND

We have started a canteen today at the Village Hall to provide hot dinners for about 30-38 children, evacuated and local, who have a long distance to come. The ladies of the Village with one or two helpers are doing this work voluntarily. We are charging 3d per head where there are two or more in a family and 4d per head for an only child.
1 NOVEMBER 1939 CLYMPING, W. SUSSEX

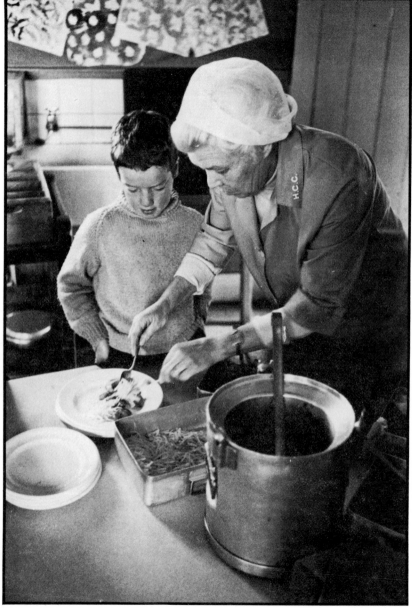

This being the anniversary of the Gunpowder Plot I gave the boys a half holiday.
5 NOVEMBER 1875 ROSEDALE ABBEY, YORKSHIRE

Paid for 8 doz Reed at 12/-
per doz to thatch school
room   £4 16 0
Paid George Bush for
Thatching school room   £2 7 6
2 JANUARY 1846 KILMERSDON, SOMERSET

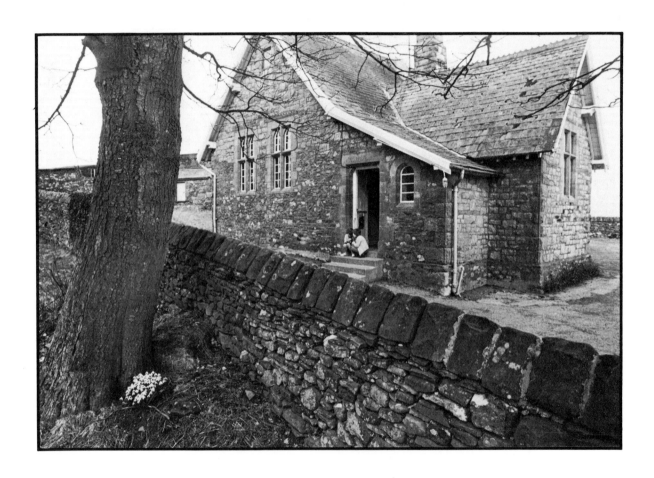

Not many children at school all the
week, gone picking cowslips for wine.
2 MAY 1883 EARL'S CROOME,
HEREFORD AND WORCESTERSHIRE

I took the boy's cricket team to
Longtoff this afternoon and they
gained another victory 45 runs and
63 for 7. Lady Sykes kindly lent me
the 'ambulance' to go in.
4 JULY 1924 SLEDMERE, HUMBERSIDE

The children have a May Queen. With decorated wands we marched round the village with many songs and dances. Collected £3 for the Lord Mayor's fund.
14 MAY 1947 CURRIDGE, BERKSHIRE

The children held their usual holiday today. After parading the village with a garland of flowers they sat down to tea, cake, bread and butter in the school room.
1 MAY 1901 BARNWELL, NORTHANTS

The children had a hay-tea at Bury Farm, having tea and games, races and rides in the hay carts. They all enjoyed themselves very much indeed and Nellie Mead thanked Mr and Mrs Compton for their kindness. Cheers were raised and then the children went home.
7 JULY 1921 SLAPTON, BUCKINGHAMSHIRE

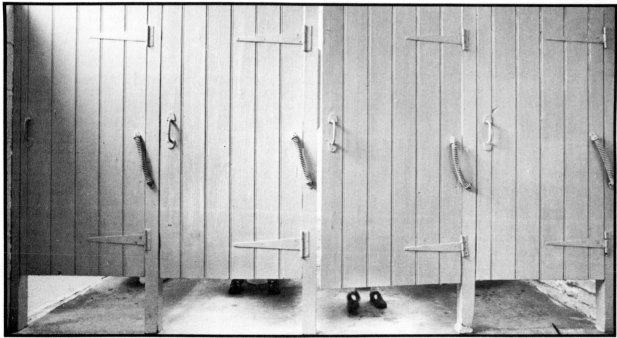

The 'bucket lavatory system' is being introduced here.
2 MAY 1912 CAMROSE SOUTH, PEMBROKESHIRE

Gas mask drill at 9.30am. During the holidays the lavatories have been converted to the earth system.
11 SEPTEMBER 1939 CAMROSE SOUTH, PEMBROKESHIRE

The office accommodation, one seat only, is hardly sufficient for fifty-four boys.
3 DECEMBER 1909 MELLS, SOMERSET

A few boys came to school this morning with rather dirty faces, one or two seemed as if they had not attempted to clean themselves. . . . were sent to the back and I saw that they gave themselves a good scrubbing in cold running water.
5 NOVEMBER 1880 WOOTTON, OXFORDSHIRE

Very cold, exercises set instead of
scripture.
5 JANUARY 1904 GLANTON,
NORTHUMBERLAND

A whist drive was again held in the
school on Friday evening . . .
Depreciation in the value of the school
plant is quite considerable . . . The
school piano has a G string broken
and the keys have quite an unnecessary
amount of candle grease smeared over
them.
4 NOVEMBER 1919 SHILBOTTLE,
NORTHUMBERLAND

Great God and wilt thou condescend
To be my father and my friend
I a poor child and thou so high
The Lord of earth and air and sky

Elizabeth Godfrey Age 12.
Bawdsey School Year 1854

This is to certify that Emily Portas was examined by **Her Majesty's Inspector** and passed in the 1st standard on June 1st 18 86.

A. Porter Hd. M.
Skegness R. S.

Miss Cartwright of Singer Sewing Machine Company called to explain the working of the Sewing Machine supplied to this school on Monday last.
9 JULY 1924 EARL'S CROOME, HEREFORD AND WORCESTERSHIRE

Large elm tree by school blown
down. The tree around which the
school children have daily played
games and sheltered from sun, wind
or rain for four and forty years.
13 FEBRUARY 1915 CLYMPING, SUSSEX

When temperature reached eighty
degrees in the shade lessons were
taken out of doors in the shade of the
trees. Desks have been carried
outside.
12 JULY 1923 SLEDMERE, HUMBERSIDE

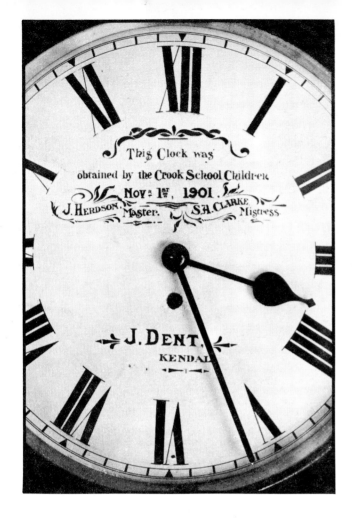

Just as school was being dismissed a bi-plane descended in the field joining school house garden. The children were intensely interested and asked the aviator a great many questions. On the arrival of the pilot with help the machine was repaired and the children had the opportunity to see the aeroplane start and to take to flight.
29 MARCH 1916 KIRBY BEDON, NORFOLK

. . . also absent, was obliged to correct him on Friday for carelessness when he kicked at me and made towards the door shouting 'I'm off home'.
18 APRIL 1882 TWYWELL, NORTHANTS

As weather is so bad and children cannot be outdoors afternoon school has started at 1.10. Lessons have been taken with only a few minutes break, instead of playtime and the children have gone home twenty minutes early. The rooms are very dark as electric light is banned.
12 MARCH 1947 CURRIDGE, BERKSHIRE

The desks are highly objectionable as they tend to make the children lazy. I may call them lounging benches.
1 AUGUST 1873 IREBY, CUMBRIA

There was no school in the afternoon. Today it is the village festival commonly called the well dressing.
10 FEBRUARY 1882 WARSLOW, STAFFORDSHIRE

Children of agricultural labourers
one child
two child } 2d each
three child
four or more   1d each

Children of carpenters, masons,
private servants
one to three 3d each
all beyond this number 2d each

Children of farmers
one to three ch. 4d each
all beyond this number 3d each
11 MAY 1874 LITTLE TEW,
OXFORDSHIRE

There is still no sign of our getting
any farmer to supply milk to this
school. There isn't even a waste piece
of land that would keep a cow.
27 FEBRUARY 1942 CHAPEL LAWN,
SHROPSHIRE

The mistress should take care that
she does not injure her health by
standing too much.
1 JULY 1878 CHAPEL LAWN,
SHROPSHIRE

Resolved that an offer of 1/6 per week
be made for sweeping school and
attending to closets.
16 DECEMBER 1884 PUNNETTS TOWN,
W. SUSSEX

A little boy . . . a late scholar of the school is being laid to rest in the churchyard this afternoon. He attended school as recently as last Thursday and today is Tuesday. He is a victim to diphtheria.
8 NOVEMBER 1910 GARTON ON THE WOLDS, HUMBERSIDE

Photographs taken of schools in the following villages

Apethorpe, Northamptonshire *11 left*
Arley, Cheshire *41 right*
Arlingham, Gloucestershire *57*
Barbon, Cumbria *34 left*
Barnwell, Northamptonshire *36 right*
Bassenthwaite, Cumbria *12 right*
Bawdsey, Suffolk *76 bottom left*
Beer, Devon *52 bottom*
Berkhamsytch, Staffordshire *24 left; 25 right*
Bethlehem, Dyfed *30 left*
Blanchland, Northumberland *9; 51 left*
Bothel, Cumbria *88 bottom*
Breamore, Hampshire *59 left*
Brough, Cumbria *67 left*
Burbage, Wiltshire *58 bottom right*
Burrough Green, Cambridgeshire *20*
Caldbeck Upton, Cumbria *12 left*
Capel Gwynfe, Dyfed *88 left*
Cardington, Bedfordshire *37 left*
Carlton le Moorland, Lincolnshire *78 left*
Castle Bytham, Lincolnshire *46; 58 top left*
Cavendish, Suffolk *19 top*
Cefn Meiriadog, Clwyd* *60 left*
Childswickham, Hereford and Worcestershire *76 bottom right*
Chislet, Kent *17 bottom left*
Clapham and Patching, West Sussex *42 right*
Clymping, West Sussex *50 bottom left*
Creeting St. Mary, Suffolk *92 right*
Croesor, Gwynedd *13*
Crook, Cumbria *51 centre right; 55 left; 81 left*
Crosby Garrett, Cumbria *74 right; 91 right*
Curridge, Berkshire *43 left*
Delamere, Cheshire *26 right*
Denton, Lincolnshire *59 right*
Derwen, Clwyd *26 left; 36 left; 44 left*
Eardisland, Hereford and Worcestershire* *60 right*
Easter Compton, Avon *35 centre*
Edenham, Lincolnshire *53 left*
Edge, Gloucestershire *18 left; 74 left*
Elan Village, Powys* *17 top left; 54 top left; 61; 80 right; 86 left*
Foxearth, Essex *21*
Glanton, Northumberland *88 right; 89*
Golden Grove, Dyfed *22 left*
Graig Bedlinog, Mid Glamorgan *45 left*
Great Bedwyn, Wiltshire *28*
Hemingford Abbots, Cambridgeshire* *63*
Hemington, Somerset *32 left*
Henham, Suffolk *55 right*
Horton, Avon *32 right*
Hovingham, North Yorkshire *10 right; 22 right*
Ilam, Staffordshire *84; front cover*
Iwerne Minster, Dorset *49*
Keevil, Wiltshire *44 right*
Kings Meaburn, Cumbria *53 right*

Kirby Bedon, Norfolk* *39 right; 50 right; 75; 81 right; 92 left; end papers*
Kirkby on Bain, Lincolnshire *25 right*
Lindale, Cumbria *16 left*
Little Bytham, Lincolnshire *50 top left*
Llandeussant, Dyfed *67 right*
Llandwrog, Gwynedd *17 right*
Llaneglwys, Powys *5*
Loders, Dorset *68*
Lupton, Cumbria *64; 71*
Madingley, Cambridgeshire *47 left; 78; 82 left; 87*
Marsh Baldon, Oxfordshire *27 top right*
Mawgan-in-Pydar, Cornwall *10 left*
Melbury Abbas, Dorset *78 right; 79 left*
Mells, Somerset *70 bottom*
Metheringham, Lincolnshire *85 right*
Michaelstowe, Cornwall* *47 right*
Milburn, Cumbria *52 top*
Nether Whitacre, Warwickshire *93 right*
Norbury, Derbyshire *18 right; 39 left; 40 bottom right*
Oakenshaw, County Durham *93 left*
Old Warden, Bedfordshire *25 centre; 48 bottom right; 91 left*
Onecote, Staffordshire *14 right; 27 left*
Parwich, Derbyshire *15*
Petham, Kent *48 top right*
Portesham, Dorset *37 right*
Powerstock, Dorset *62*
Preston Bissett, Buckinghamshire *68 right*
Rhiwlas, Gwynedd *16 right; 40 left*
Rickinghall Inferior, Suffolk *54 top right*
Rosedale Abbey, North Yorkshire *90 right*
St. George, Clwyd *80 left*
St. Neot, Cornwall *11 right*
Sandford, Devon *23*
Sellack, Hereford and Worcestershire *94*
Sheen, Staffordshire *31; 33*
Sledmere, Humberside *42 left*
Stoke by Clare, Suffolk *27 bottom right*
Stokesby, Norfolk* *1; 14 left; 29 bottom right; 30 right; 34 right; 35 right; 65; 86 right; back cover*
Sutterton, Lincolnshire *73*
Swanbourne, Buckinghamshire *69*
Symondsbury, Dorset *45 right*
Temple Sowerby, Cumbria *29 top right*
Thornborough, Buckinghamshire *72 right*
Trethosa, Cornwall *66*
Turvey, Bedfordshire *19 bottom*
Twywell, Northamptonshire* *32 centre*
Ufford, Suffolk *70 top*
Upper Slaughter, Gloucestershire *72 right*
Upton St. Leonards, Gloucestershire *38 left; 54 bottom right*
Warmington, Cheshire *41 left; 51 top left; 82 right; 83*
Waterfall, Staffordshire *38 right*
Waunfawr, Gwynedd *55 centre*

Welton le Marsh, Lincolnshire *51 bottom right; 76 top left; 79 right*
West Lavington, West Sussex *85 left*
Whippingham, Isle of Wight *58 bottom left*
Wigtoft, Lincolnshire* *58 top right*
Winton, Cumbria *56 right*
Witham-on-the-Hill, Lincolnshire *29 left; 35 left*
Wormbridge, Hereford and Worcestershire *43 right*
Wortham Long Green, Suffolk *48 left*
Wray-with-Botton, Lancashire *40 top right; 56 left; 90 left*

* denotes school closed before publication